YASMINE BEN SALMI

I THINK

I LOST MY

HAPPINESS

JOURNEYING WITH **FAITH**,
ONE PRAYER AT A TIME.

**The Choice
is Yours**
PUBLISHING

I THINK I LOST MY HAPPINESS

Published by The Choice Is Yours Publishing

Copyright © 2025 Yasmine Ben Salmi

The author asserts the moral right under the Copyright, Designs and Patents Act 1988 to be identified as the author of this work.

Copyright © 2025 Yasmine Ben Salmi
Interior and cover design by Lashai Ben Salmi
All rights reserved.

Paperback ISBN: 978-1-915862-25-9
Hardback ISBN: 978-1-915862-24-2

YASMINE BEN SALMI

I THINK
I LOST MY
HAPPINESS

JOURNEYING WITH **FAITH**, **ONE PRAYER** AT A TIME.

" Happiness
lives inside
your heart

INTRODUCTION

INTRODUCTION

Lila Johnson had always been a bright and cheerful girl, full of laughter and curiosity. She loved exploring the world around her, spending time with her friends, and finding joy in the little things. But one sunny Monday morning, as she sat up in her bed, she felt a strange emptiness. It was as if a piece of her heart had gone missing.

"I think I lost my happiness," she whispered to herself.

Determined to find it again, Lila embarked on a journey that would take her to unexpected places and teach her valuable lessons about life. She searched high and low, in the most obvious and the most unusual places. Along the way, her five closest friends joined her in the quest, each bringing their unique perspective and support.

For 365 days, Lila's search for happiness led her through laughter and tears, frustration and enlightenment. She discovered that happiness wasn't something you could find under a bed, in a classroom, or even in the most thrilling adventures. Instead, she learned that happiness is a state of being, a choice that comes from within.

Join Lila on her heartfelt journey as she uncovers the true essence of happiness, guided by gratitude, respect, kindness, love, and empathy. Through her story, you'll discover that sometimes, what you're searching for has been inside you all along.

CHAPTER 1: THE SEARCH BEGINS

Lila Johnson woke up on a sunny Monday morning with a strange feeling in her heart.

Something was missing, and she couldn't quite put her finger on it.

As she sat up in her
bed, she muttered,

"I think I lost my happiness"

Determined to find it, she started by looking under her bed.

Dust bunnies and old toys stared back at her.

"Nope, not here," she sighed.

Today was the first day of her search for happiness, and she decided

she'd better get
ready for school.

CHAPTER 2:
SCHOOL DAZE

At school, Lila confided in her best friend, Emma.

"I think I lost
my
happiness,"
she explained
during lunch.

Emma, with her usual
cheerful demeanour,
said,

"Maybe you left it in the art room! Let's go check after class."

They searched the art room high and low, but all they found were paint splatters and crumpled papers.

Lila felt a bit empty. Emma hugged her and said, "Don't worry, we'll find it."

YASMINE BEN SALMI

I THINK
I LOST MY
HAPPINESS

JOURNEYING WITH **FAITH**,
ONE PRAYER AT A TIME.

CHAPTER 3: THE QUEST CONTINUES

For the next week, Lila's friends joined the search. Henry, the energy of the class,

suggested they look for
happiness in laughter.

They spent the
afternoon
telling jokes
and giggling.

It was fun, but when Lila got home, she still felt the same emptiness.

Next, Zara, the
bookworm, brought her
a stack of books.

"Maybe happiness is in a story," she suggested.

Lila read through adventures and mysteries,

but although she enjoyed them, happiness didn't return.

YASMINE BEN SALMI

I THINK
I LOST MY
HAPPINESS

JOURNEYING WITH **FAITH,**
ONE PRAYER AT A TIME.

CHAPTER 4:
THE
REFLECTION

Two weeks passed, and Lila felt more lost than ever.

One day, as she sat in
the park with Mia,

the nature lover, Mia
said,

"Happiness is in the beauty around us."

They walked among the flowers and trees, and though it was peaceful, Lila's heart remained heavy.

Then came David, the athlete. "Maybe happiness is in activity," he proposed.

They played soccer and ran races.

The exercise
was
exhilarating,
but the hole in
Lila's heart
persisted.

YASMINE BEN SALMI

I THINK
I LOST MY
HAPPINESS

JOURNEYING WITH **FAITH**,
ONE PRAYER AT A TIME.

CHAPTER 5:
A MONTH OF
SEARCHING

A month into her search, Lila began to despair. "What if I never find my happiness?" she thought.

She tried new hobbies,
talked to new people,
and even asked

her teachers for advice. Everyone had suggestions, but nothing seemed to work.

CHAPTER 6:
THE YEAR OF
DISCOVERY

Days turned into months, and soon a year had passed. Lila had searched everywhere she could think of.

She had explored
laughter, stories,
nature, activity, and
more.

She had become kinder,
more respectful, and
more compassionate,

but the elusive
happiness
seemed beyond
her reach.

One evening, sitting by herself, Lila reflected on her journey.

She thought about all the things she had tried and all the people who had helped her.

Slowly, she began to realize something profound.

CHAPTER 7: THE REVELATION

The next day, Lila gathered her friends.

"I need to tell you something," she said.

"I've spent a
whole year
looking for
happiness.

I looked
under my
bed, at
school,

in laughter, stories,
nature, and sports.

I asked everyone for help.

And do you know what I found?"

Her friends leaned in, curious.

"I found that happiness isn't something you find outside of yourself.

It's something you choose
to feel inside.

Finding one's happiness often involves a combination of internal and external factors.

Here are some key components:

Self-Awareness:

- Understanding your values, desires, strengths, and weaknesses.

- Reflecting on what truly matters to you and what makes you feel fulfilled.

Gratitude:

- Practicing gratitude by regularly acknowledging and appreciating the positive aspects of your life.

- Keeping a gratitude journal to remind yourself of things you are thankful for.

Positive Relationships:
- Building and maintaining meaningful relationships with family, friends, and community.

- Surrounding yourself with supportive, positive people who uplift and encourage you.

Purpose and Goals:
- Setting and working towards personal and professional goals.

- Having a sense of purpose or direction in life that motivates and inspires you.

Mindfulness and Presence:
- Practicing mindfulness to stay present in the moment and reduce stress.

- Engaging in activities like meditation, yoga, or deep-breathing exercises.

Self-Compassion and
Acceptance:
- Being kind and
  forgiving to yourself,
  especially in times of
  failure or difficulty.

- Accepting yourself as you are and acknowledging your worth.

Healthy Lifestyle:
- Maintaining physical health through regular exercise, a balanced diet, and sufficient sleep.

- Taking care of your mental health by managing stress and seeking help when needed.

Acts of Kindness and Service:
- Helping others and contributing to the well-being of your community.

- Volunteering or performing random acts of kindness, which can boost your own sense of happiness.

Balance and Flexibility:
- Balancing different aspects of your life, such as work, leisure, and relationships.

- Being flexible and adaptable to change and challenges.

Continuous Learning
and Growth:
- Engaging in lifelong
  learning and
  personal
  development.

- Exploring new interests, skills, and experiences that stimulate and satisfy you.

Combining these
elements can create
a foundation for
lasting happiness
and well-being."
Emma smiled.

"So, you found it after all?"Lila nodded.

"Yes, I think I did. It was inside me all along.

I just needed to choose to be happy."

YASMINE BEN SALMI

I THINK
I LOST MY
HAPPINESS

JOURNEYING WITH **FAITH**,
ONE PRAYER AT A TIME.

CHAPTER 8:
A NEW
BEGINNING

With her newfound understanding, Lila embraced each day with gratitude and kindness.

She respected herself and others, showed love and compassion,

and led with empathy.
And as she did,

she realised that happiness
was no longer something
she had to search for,

because she learned that happiness is something she simply had to choose to live.

From that day on, Lila never lost her happiness again.

She carried
it with her,
in her heart,

knowing that true happiness comes from within and is nurtured by the choices we make every day.

And so, her
journey
didn't end;

it had just begun.

YASMINE BEN SALMI

I THINK
I LOST MY
HAPPINESS

JOURNEYING WITH **FAITH,**
ONE PRAYER AT A TIME.

ABOUT THE
AUTHOR

ABOUT The AUTHOR

Purpose: To eradicate low self-esteem by liberating 1 million young people through the teaching of self love

Website: https://linktr.ee/YasmineBenSalmi

Guest speaker at the Global Black Impact Summit founded by the legendary Clarence Seedorf Chairman, Black Impact Foundation: https://globalblackimpact.com/speakers-2023/

Yasmine is a proud member of the Association of Surgeons of Great Britain and Ireland and The British Association of Black Surgeons, which is the UK's largest body of Black surgical professionals.

Proud contributor alongside my four siblings at the UN SOTF Youth Consultations:

Guest speaker at Equinix "Global Happiness Speaker Series":

Yasmine published a scientific article with her mentor Detina Zalli who's a lead professor from Harvard, Oxford and Cambridge: https://oxfordacademy.io/overview-of-reconstructive-plastic-surgery-advantages-and-disadvantages/

Yasmine is a co-host alongside her siblings Lashai and Paolo Ben Salmi for this years NGO Whisper Summit 2022: https://ngowhisperer.com/summit/

BEN SALMI FAMILY MANTRA

"BEN SALMI TEAMWORK MAKES THE DREAMWORK

We believe that there is no such thing as failure, only feedback.

We also believe that the journey of one thousand miles begins with a single step in the right direction

FAMILY ANTHEM

If you want to be somebody,
If you want to go somewhere,
You better wake up and PAY ATTENTION

I'm ready to be somebody,
I'm ready to go somewhere,
I'm ready to wake up and PAY ATTENTION!

The question is ARE YOU?

Let's STAY CONNECTED

HTTPS://LINKTR.EE/YASMINEBENSALMI

in Yasmine Ben Salmi

⊙ @AuthorYasmineBenSalmi

✉ info@dreamingbigtogether.com

," **HAPPINESS LIVES IN YOUR HEART**

YASMINE BEN SALMI

I THINK
I LOST MY
HAPPINESS

JOURNEYING WITH **FAITH**,
ONE PRAYER AT A TIME.